T0197459

Sir Dwight And the House of Ight

"A story using the ight family of words"

Story: Rachel Ohtani
Pictures: Aiko Ohtani Jilek

To order additional copies of this book, contact:
Xlibris
1-888-795-4274
www.Xlibris.com
Orders@Xlibris.com

ISBN: Softcover   978-1-4500-8833-6

Library of Congress Control Number: 2010905649

Print information available on the last page

Rev. date: 02/19/2020

One night a Knight named Dwight
rode by the House of Ight.

It was to his delight that he caught sight of Lady Ight. She stood in the window of greatest height.

She started to scream with all her might.

Then she saw a Knight in the night.
"What a welcome sight you are Sir Dwight."
"Please help me in my plight. There is a
fight right at this height."

14

Sir Dwight jumped off his horse. He quickly ran up the flight of stairs to the greatest height. In the dim light he could see a slight figure tied tight to a post.

16

Then Sir Ight walked in the bright room. He had a slight wound on his right eye, but mostly he was frightened.

"I came to help you in your plight," said Sir Dwight.

"It was a slight fight," said Ight.

"Sir Wright was trying to steal my freight at eight o'clock."

"But to my delight I gave a good fight. Now I'm alright!"

"But please Sir Dwight don't fight in the night without a light; you might frighten your wife."

"Good night."

Questions

1. On a sheet of paper list all the "ight" words in this story.

2. Find two words in this story that end in ight but are not pronounced (it). Can you think of any reason why these words do not rhyme with the others.

   1.   2.

3. List as many ight words as you can think of using suffixes and prefixes.

4. Choose another list of rhyming words and write your own story.

   - And

   - Ice

   - Ake

   - Ink

   - Ive

   - Ame